Dotty's Art

by Kama Einhorn
illustrated by Barb Dragony

Scott Foresman
is an imprint of

Glenview, Illinois • Boston, Massachusetts • Chandler, Arizona
Upper Saddle River, New Jersey

Photographs

Every effort has been made to secure permission and provide appropriate credit for photographic material. The publisher deeply regrets any omission and pledges to correct errors called to its attention in subsequent editions.

Unless otherwise acknowledged, all photographs are the property of Pearson Education, Inc.

Photo locators denoted as follows: Top (T), Center (C), Bottom (B), Left (L), Right (R), Background (Bkgd)

12 Peter Horree/Alamy Images.

Illustrations Barbara Dragony.

ISBN 13: 978-0-328-50832-7
ISBN 10:   0-328-50832-2

After science class, Dotty sat at her desk and listened to her teacher, Mr. Dean, talk about a school art show. Each student could enter one piece of art.

Dotty started to think. Bill said he'd draw his team playing soccer. Dotty told Maria that she should enter her pretty, clay turtle. But sadly, Dotty had no idea for her own art.

At home, Dotty worried. She couldn't even guess what she would create.

Her mom said, "How about painting an apple tree?"

Her dad asked, "Can you draw using your name?"

"What do you mean?" asked Dotty.

"Do you remember when we went to the art show?" asked dad.

Mom added, "Remember the painter you called the dot artist?"

"Seurat. I liked him a lot! I think I said that over and over. Yes, I remember!" laughed Dotty.

"Start drawing dots, Dotty," Dad said.

Dotty liked the idea. She knew she could do it.

Dotty took crayons, markers, and a giant piece of paper, and started dotting away. She made big dots, little dots, and dots of every color. She filled her paper with thousands of dots. It took all week.

Finally, she finished. There was a little dot village, little dot bees and fleas, and little dot people eating dot peas. The people even wore little dot shoes.

"It's pretty," Dotty thought. "I'll call it *Dotty's Dots.*"

At the school art show Dotty drank punch and looked at her friends' art. Jean had painted a real wagon wheel in all different colors. Dan had drawn one of his dreams.

Dotty liked to watch everyone look at her dots.

Then her mom came over. "*Dotty's Dots* won a blue ribbon," she said.

"We always knew your name would come in handy someday!" Dotty's dad laughed.

Georges Seurat

In the story, Dotty says she likes the "dot artist" Seurat. Georges Seurat was born in Paris, France, in 1859. He began drawing while he was in school. The style of painting he created used tiny "points" or dots of paint. He thought that using color this way helped show how light changes what we see.